GHOST TANTRAS

GHOST TANTRAS

Michael McClure

City Lights | Grey Fox
San Francisco

Cover photograph by Wallace Berman, courtesy of the Estate of Wallace
Berman and Michael Kohn Gallery, Los Angeles
Makeup by Robert Lavigne

Library of Congress Cataloging-in-Publication Data
McClure, Michael.
Ghost Tantras / Michael McClure.
    pages cm
ISBN 978-0-87286-627-0 (pbk.)
I. Title.
PS3563.A262G46 2013
811'.54—dc23

                                2013020599

City Lights Books are published at the City Lights Bookstore,
261 Columbus Avenue, San Francisco, CA 94133.
www.citylights.com

This book is dedicated
to the Human Spirit & all Mammals.

Many decades ago in San Francisco, lying on the couch, reading the newly written first Ghost Tantra as it unveiled to my eyes and ears, I feel a ripple, maybe a shudder, of embarrassment and laugh at myself. Where is the beauty that I expect after my experience of that ball of silence promising me ninety-nine tantras to the goddess? I remember Robert Creeley's admonition to believe in the experience of writing the poem. I look at the page again — it brings love looking for sugar! I know that there are to be ninety-eight more of these. I'm sure of it.

The next day Ghost Tantra 2 appears and speaks in "beast language" . . . the Tantra waves baby arms at me and gives me news of the great Tibetan poet Milarepa who is imprinting himself on the poem, becoming a "mystic experience" — and tells me that everything lies in front of me not in the past. Yes, it is a mystic experience and is my self-experience which can be laughable as easily as loaded with torment. Maybe some beauty that I do not expect will occur in a different guise or body or body of words. Next, Ghost Tantra 3 brings its own announcement with a cigar and cherries, and the sounds that begin to feel familiar — "grooooooooor yahh-yort gahhr."

Immediately afterward, Tantra 4 carries long howls, brings gardens with cool shadows, and sings of youth and liberation. Sounds of the molecular body account for the fifth Tantra. Tantra 8 has the rose and lily-lovely cheek of the goddess appearing. Belief is beginning to push the edge of dubiety back.

Tantra 13 begins, "OH LOVELY LINE BETWEEN DAY AND DREAM." I am "pleased and richly placid," I am sentient and this flow of language seems to be conscious, and is its own being. Can these, in fact, bring changes to the universe, as tantras should do? I'm changing.

Once comic books had words like "CLANG" and the ancient Greek poem says "KLANG." Did Goethe write *Faust* or did Faust create Goethe?

I am excited with the existence coming into being — I have brought it about.

—∽—

Now it is time to pack my bag for the air flight to Mexico City and the long drive to Huautla de Jiménez — and the journey into the mountains of Oaxaca.

I write Tantra 15b in my notebook as the plane departs San Francisco for Mexico City. I have no idea what I'm doing — just writing. I sit in the near empty plane with a swelling sense of meditation, feeling the plane's metal walls shudder with thoughtless physical pleasure. Above a central California of the Sixties I am thrilled with the magic entering Tantra 16. By the time the plane lands in Mexico City there is little doubt left. In the airport the sadness of all of everything strengthens me.

We drive across the desert stopping sometimes to look at roadside botany. Hours later, we turn off the worn asphalt and enter the mountains into an adventure of thunder and lightning storms and deserted, roadside, cliff edges and narrower "trails" with pounding torrents crushing them — no campesino or burro to be seen in the steep craggy latenight flashes of a landslide drive. Waking in the morning in the small pueblo of Huautla de Jiménez, in a quieter rain, we drive from the country town to empty cow pastures and carefully make cultures of *psilocybes*, sterilizing the instruments with a portable burner, propping a tarp of waterproof canvas over our heads, and our sterilized instruments make clean cuts in the small mushrooms. In the early afternoon the *curandera* Maria Sabina allows us into her chanting ceremony. Lightning is flashing and thunder booming through the uncovered windows of her home on a high road. Later that day carrying our broken movie camera, we listen to the stories of Isauro Nave, a *curandero* of the Leaves of the Good Shepherdess, in his hacienda. A few days later, we are in a rural Mexican airport and begin flying to San Francisco.

At home, in a flat overlooking the Golden Gate and waves crashing on Point Bonita, I resume writing the Tantras. About this time I struggle in my writing with my shyness and an urge to explore self-dramatization — to attempt a non-mimetic poetry which would not be descriptive of the ordinary world but would be at one with creation of muscular music coming from the body and organs and inspiring sounds and "pictures" from that source.

I believe that a poem I make is part of myself like an organ or spirit-body, and these poem-tantras are becoming a body and growing up — having a life of their own. This is not hard to imagine for a young poet who believes in the divinity of Blake and Shelley, and in the paintings of Clyfford Still and Jackson Pollock as a part of those artists' being.

It was, and is, part of my art to believe that all conceptions of boundaries are lies . . .

As the Tantras move forward and as the ball of silence from which they sound-out is both more clear and more elusive, I consider them carefully. I can feel the spirit of Marilyn Monroe (Tantra 39) entering them the day after her death in 1962. It is only right; it is a business of the goddess. I like the mammalian music when I declaim the poem. Now the title occurs to me "Ghost" from the German "Geist" or soul — Spirit Tantras — Ghost Tantras. I am moved by Brahms' Four Serious Songs as they sing, in German, the Preacher of the Old Testament's concern with the spirit of men and the spirit of the beasts and how one goes down under the earth and the other goes out, out, out. Huge low silences and huge high silences are occurring. Tantra 49, "SILENCE THE EYES! BECALM THE SENSES!" has an extending and extended life.

A year or two later, Bruce Conner and I go to the San Francisco Zoo to record lion roars and snow leopard growls for a sound-play I have written. The newly published first edition of this book is in my back pocket and through a lucky event we end up in the lion house, and I yell this Tantra to the four maned males of the building. They roar back with me and we sing it together. The five of us are deeply pleased; also I am profoundly shaken and then shaken again when Bruce plays back the tape he made with his high fidelity machine. A few years later a public television group is making documentary films of the new generation of poets and asks me to read again to the lions and again they roar with me. The film was shown on TV and now it can be found on the internet.

From Ghost Tantra 90 on, the stanzas build to power and the final ones close by hugely shouting into the dense mattress-like curtain of material reality, until it begins to lift in tranquility.

Michael McClure
Oakland, 2013

You've never heard anything like this before. These are my personal songs but anyone can sing them. Pronounce them as they are spelled and don't worry about details — use a natural voice and let the vibrations occur. They come from a swirling ball of silence that melds with outer sounds and thought. They were written in kitchens and bedrooms and frontrooms and airplanes, and a couple in Mexico City. Their purpose is to bring beauty and change the shape of the universe.

I WAS HERE AND I LIKED IT !
It was all O.K.
I suffered.
There were scents, and flowers, and textures, beautiful women.
I was a handsome man. I invented love.
I radiated genius for those who saw me with loving eyes.
I was happy — I laughed and cried. Constantly new
sights and sounds. I trembled and sweated
at the sight of beauty. I laughed at strong
things because I loved them — wanting to kick them in
and make freedom. When I go I'M GONE.
Don't resurrect me
or the duplicates of my atoms.
It was perfect !
I am sheer spirit.

Poetry is a muscular principle and a revolution for the body-spirit and intellect and ear. Making images and pictures, even when speaking with melody, is not enough. There must be a poetry of pure beauty and energy that does not mimic but joins and exhorts reality and states the daily higher vision. To dim the senses and to listen to inner energies a-roar is sometimes called the religious experience. It does not matter what it is called. Laughter as well as love is passion. The loveliness the nose snuffs in air may be translated to sound by interior perceptive organs. The touch of velvet on the fingertips may become a cry when time is stopped. Speed like calmness may become a pleasure or gentle muffled sound. A dahlia or fern might become pure speech in meditation. A woman's body might become the sound of worship. A goddess lies coiled at the base of man's body, and pure tantric sound might awaken her. There are no laws but living changing ones, and any system is a touch of death.

Read these poems as you would Lorca, or Mayakovsky, or Lawrence but READ ALOUD AND SING THEM.

—⚉—

These are spontaneous stanzas published in the order and with the natural sounds in which they were first written. If there is an "OOOOOOOOOOOOOOOH" simply say a long loud "oooh". If there is a "gahr" simply say gar and put an h in.

Look at stanza 51. It begins in English and turns into beast language — star becomes stahr. Body becomes boody. Nose becomes noze. Everybody knows how to pronounce NOH or VOOR-NAH or GAHROOOOO ME.

Pronounce sounds as they are spelled and don't worry about details — let individual pronunciations and vibrations occur and don't look for secret meanings. Read them aloud and there will be more pleasure.

IN AIR, IN AIR BLUE OP PINK STREAK
I HEAR ME YOU,
DOOOOOODOOOOOR GHROOO OOO OH.
Dooo est mah noo ehh, HO, grahhhr,
RAHHR
GRAHHHS HAHRR-gahrooooooooooooh.
Dream refuge of air hair neeoooobless.
Oh bleeeeeze nooo art,
Seee lite im dumm breth fett haw-gra.
!! SHAKE-ZAY BOTH !!
Reeeen Mooo art gohbay the tynor jahr-
dooeeeee
sharr starr blimm bobrekk nokcrog,
Zooney Leeert!
BWOOOO.OH! HAHHR! NDOOOOOOOOOOO
weep.
Bless my love yoo sollidd
weep.

Ghost Tantra (17)

(0 in central
calif at night-beginning)

Facsimile of manuscript of Ghost Tantra seventeen

GHOST TANTRAS

GOOOOOOR ! GOOOOOOOOOO !
GOOOOOOOOOOR !
GRAHHH ! GRAHH ! GRAHH !
Grah gooooor ! Ghahh ! Graaarr ! Greeeeer ! Grayowhr !
Greeeeee
GRAHHRR ! RAHHR ! GRAGHHRR ! RAHR !
RAHR ! RAHHR ! GRAHHHR ! GAHHR ! HRAHR !
BE NOT SUGAR BUT BE LOVE
looking for sugar !
GAHHHHHHHH !
ROWRR !
GROOOOOOOOOOH !

PLEASURE FEARS ME, FOOT ROSE, FOOT BREATH,
BY BLAHHR MOKGROOOOOOO TARRR
nowp tytath brooooooooooooooooooooo

—

In the middle of the night I dreamed I was a creature
like the great Tibetan Yogi Milarepa.
I sang a song beginning :
"Home lies in front of you not in the past.
Follow your nose
to it."
It had great mystic import, both apparent and hidden.
I was pleased with it.
GOOOOOOOOOOR !
GROOOOOOOOOOOOOOOOOOOOH !
GOOOOOOOO.
ROOOOOOOOOOOH !
POWFF ! RAHH ! BLAHHR !

SREEEEEEEEEEEEEE GROWWVRR
WHEEEET YAHH !
YAHHHH ! YAHHHH ! YAHHHHYEE!
Grooooooooooor grooooooooooor
grooooooooor yahh-yort gahhr
strawberry-peach darkness in daylight pale flesh brain.
Grahhroooh ! Moooor tannyahr. Grahh ! Shaktigroor
varmdama grooor. Vyrahhr grahh grahhh graa-rrrrr !
Pleasing light taste gahhveeeeeeeeee brooooooooooo.
LITTLE GIRL EYES. LITTLE GIRL EYES.
RADIANT SNORT.
CIGAR.
GROOOOOOOOOOOOH.
GROOOOOOOOOOOOO — OOH.
GROOOOOOOOOOOOOOH GRAHHH ! GYEEE.
Cherries.

DOORWAYS ARE BARE GARDENS OF COOL
SHADOWS !
ENTRANCEWAYS ARE GARDENS OF FUTURITY !
GAHROOOOOOOOOOOOOOOOOOOOOOOOH !
GAHROOOOOOOOOOOOOOOOOOOOOOOOOH !
We memorized the remembrances of our sexuality
— holding hands with our heads in the opposite directions.
All of our dearness returned.
We are youthful again
and liberated ! LIBERATED !
In the morn I saw the coold doorways & entrances
through the colorful real true myth of the night.
KROOOOOOOOOOOL-MRIST,
grooooooooooorfreeeeeeeeeee
above greye-kra!
Sweeting. Sweetling !

(for Kaera)

BRAHHNG ! KROOOR BRATOOOOOOTH-MAR
GRRRRRRRRRAHH ! GROOOOOOOR !
Swow mownarr grah roooooooh muhr
zneeeeeeeeeeeeeeeesweeeeeee bwooooooo
mooombwattah lah lah gwahr grrrrrrrrr
BWEEE NOOOOOOOOOO !
GOOOOOOOOOOOOOOOOOOOOOO;
sweeepie joooo nahg gar drrrrr twi
chengreeoooo grrrrrrrrrrr gowld snarrr
mrooooooooooooooo-wub
WUB
WUB
WUB
WUB
WUB
WUB
WUB
bweeeeeeeeee.

GRAHGG ! KROOOOOOPROOOOO
GROOOOOOOOOOOH.
Profiles of beautiful women making a veil
of shimmers and features of smiles upon all beings.
ME!
ME ! ME ! ME ! ME ! GROOOOOOOOOOOOOOR !
MEGROOOOOOOOOR, ME SERMON GROOOO.
Me from everything to gray. Me see
nooooor tha kiss me groooooor.

Here is a groo finger.

GHHHROOOOOO GAHROOOOOOO EEEKA CAR,
cargroooooooo longkarr GRAHHH !
Cowmroooooose blooooo mewie-weeeep.
VOOOOOOOOOOOO?
Shgrarr? Yagabb krahr yellow vipt
mwooo? Swoooooooooooooo lub byeeee bwack meee !
MAKE LOVE SOUNDS.
HERE SMELL.
Grahh pallid ! Graaah love nowhr
bwooooooooo krahh noooo-boooooose !
Saba-grooooh stahr zaboth mwoooo
kakra graaaah grahh grrrrrrrr
mweeeeeeeee melt.

Awaken grahhh nameless brahh beauty brahhh sense :
SENZOR BRAHH-GRAHH GROOOOOWEE !
Hrrruh ! Rahhr. Gragma huhrr vreeeemagtarb.
OH !
Ohhhh ooooie more superb than Anita Ekberg.
YOU !
Proud cones of Grecian breasts
and thighs and belly. Smile in the darkness.
Groooooooooooooooh ! Gooooooor
mowkarg-lang vooooo mahh tah.
Rose and lily lovely cheek mate;
GROOOOOOOOOOOOO
OOOOOOOOOOIE
Gooooooooor. HRAHH !

MWAHH!! GWOOOOOOOOOOOOO GRAH! GROOO!
Mirn-bwa gweeeek grrhhaa nar narrrrrr.
BWEEEEEEEEEEEE
Voooostarr znoch! Grahh. Grooooooor marnok sprite by gooor nokk nort bweeee fwahhh.
Gooooold blooob gine fwahr hedd ahh!
!OOOOOOH-AHH-OOOOH.
Gra-nooort bite meeegahh nooorgathtase larchk reeeeeeeze oooop Kuhnda, bweh Kuhnda dahllah bythe zvieee fooooong
KWETT MOOOOM MANOOOO GAH-
ROOOOOOOOOOOOOOOOOOOOOOOH!!
Me.
Indian. Fahhrrr.

Jahnwu ghrurr mrahh, hrehh, mrehhh, ghhraaaaa.
Rayaowh wrhehh hrmrooowgh grayoww !
Grahh ! Nhahr ! Moooorgk nahtrap zabah
mreck froooo oooh neee magwieeer voooh.
Mreeet-dahh veel !
Bweee inn dahhr hrahh hehh hroooo noweeega . . .
USE LIP !
Nooogwahh bweeeee-now-tag nye-gow-ahn
! GRAH !
SNAR ! FWAHH ! MEK ! NOHR ! KRAHH !
KRUH !
Mwoooooooooooooooooooooooo.
Grooooooooooooooooooooooooooh !
Weeeee-dooooo.

Goddesh rahnn mee nye torr nuh vah gahh.
GODDESH BWEEEN GRRHH-H-H-H-H
neehr goooo zvann tak-tag-korr mruhhr nooh.
Mwaaaaaaaaaah bleeeeeeth vroom-boz
gahh. Shaybow klah groooo. Grahh !
Mahndrahl.
Soweee noh-hoon trahng *shahr* BHROOOOH !
SMEL-GOOOHL.
Keeeeeeeeeeeeeeez mweh-nye-boo.
BLASSAH
!
Mweeeeeeeh
blech.
HROOOOOOOOOOOHN !
— Goddesh.
End-noooon

SWAHRR GRAHH GROOOOOOH GROOOOOOOH.
Revelation of eve dropping sweetly
and grahh lightly.
LITEGROOOOOOOOOR, LITE GRAHH !
Where you me who grah NAHHR !
Ahh-ooooh weeeeb being swoom.
Swoooom-grooooor bweeeeth ! Grahhgrr. Rhhagrr !
Dreeem kidden broooo. Kye ! Swooor
GRAHHR ! GRAHHR ! GRAHHR HRAGK !
Escape escape forbidden nogdoooorn.
TURQUOISE
Glahhhhh !
Twarqweeese legg.
Mur.
Lambkin.

OH LOVELY LINE BETWEEN DAY AND DREAM.
We slip over and under thee
when we are pleased and richly placid.
REFUGE FOR ALL SENTIENT BEINGS!
WHO ART THOU, I, ME?
HOOOOOOO! HOOOOOO! GRAHH!
GROOOOOOOOOH! GROOOOOH! NAHHR
MHEE!
RRGAHH!
Grooor Kayve.
MWAHH!
Greeeeeeeeee-groooooo.
GARHRRROOOOOOOOOOOOOH
WHOOG KLOWBB.
(What is not sentient? But I — more than all —
am a whole full universe.)
FULL. MAKE GROOOOR.

BWAHHH MORN-DRIFT HELD IN PASSAGE
GRAHHR !   GRAHHR !
GAHROOOOOOOOOOOOOOOOOOOOOOOOOOH ! !
Dreeem nooothowgeeii. Brooooon. Grahh !
Goooor. GOOOOR ! Gooor. Hrahhrr. Mrahh.
NOH. DREEEM. HOHH !
Mrooooooh !
Vooooo weeet gellldd.

THE TREES ARE ELEPHANTS' HEADS.
The brown whorls of hair at the top of your head.
The trees are gray-green grooooor greyeeee.
AMM SOOOTEEE AIEE ! GAROOOOOOOOOOH.
Gragg. Hrahhrr mok now-toony. Bwooooooh.
Groooor. MARRRR ! GROOOOH ! Grooooooor.
GAHROOOOOOOOOOOOOOOOOOOOOOH !
GAHROOOOOOOOOOOOOOOOOOOOOH !
MOMM.
Hraghhrr.
GROOOOOOOOH !
Mowk-towr-noowth-own-eii !
FACE,
TUSK,
WHAHHH !
GAHHROOOOOOOO ! !
LUKK !

HRAHH ! GRAHHR ! WRAH! GROOOOOOOOOOO !
BEEEEYAIRE MWAHH HRR-R-R-R-R-R-R
Frooooo mwahh tooogartooniee hrrrrrr noooor
by you come back here me nye too thoh !
SHRAHH ! SHRAHH !
WEERBNOOOR, HUHFWOOOO, HREHHHH,
oh I miss you, love, you here with bree reth
gahnoor bye weeb-doo lagg brekk-artnotty,
BWOOOOO,
WEEB TERR,
but me hool voo narg narr.

(over San Francisco)

16

SHREEE GROOO REPT HOLE MWAK-KARTERB
ROOOOHH ! — ROOOOH ! — ROOOOOH !

Meee noo lobb neee pink blue gray whirr
chooo ! Grene eeeze me vohh neer
spake sri narr bwakk meee clowd.
Siller kam bwooo mee ! Groooh teer weeept . . .
Bahd veee hool geed. Gahroooooooh ! ROOOOH !
HOOOOOOOOOORHAHH !
HOOOO-ROOOOOOH WU !
Bwahh noo meeeeee, derr veeept ah-ooh.
Jarr-shak virr gray blue, blooo, waggt
beee-stertt. I dreamed you eyes awake, hole you
toes soft. Goodbye forbidden emptiness.
YOU.
MAKE.
ME.
BIG.
ME solid hrahh grey radiance oooh !

(over central California at dusk)

IN AIR, IN AIR BLUE OF PINK STREAK, I HEAR ME
YOU —
DOOOOOOOOOOOR GHROOOOOOOH.
Dooo est mah noo ehh, HO, grahhhr, RAHHR.
GRAHHH ! HAHRR-gahrooooooooooooh.
Dream refuge of air, hair, neeoooobless.
Oh bleeeeeze nooo art.
See lite in dimm breth frett harr-gra.
!! SHAKE-ZAYBOTH !!
Reeem nooo art gohbaythe tynor jahr drooeeeee
sharr starr blimm bobrekk nokcrog. Zooneye deeert !
BWOOOOOH ! HAHHR ! NOOOOOOO-
OOO
weep.
Bless my love you sollidd
weep.

(o'er central California at night-beginning)

A UNIVERSE OF ENERGETIC STILLNESS. ME NA
THOOOR OOH
CALM ME I AM ROOOOOHRR AND CALM
still rahoooor ! Theee la aye ah oh hrooo hmm mahh.
Pure white, glow-white hallway & figures romance human
technicolor.
WOO-OOOOOOOOOOOOO-
GAHH-roooooooor.
DRAH !-DRAH !-DRAH !-DRAH !-DRAH !-DRAH !
Here me I am you big hraaa deeer fur, blue green feather
am gooor white.
GROOHH !   ! GROOHH
                ! NOHH !
GROOHH !   ! GROOHH

(on leaving Los Angeles)

RED BLACK, BLUE BLACK, PURPLE BLACK, BLUE.
ORANGE DAWN O'ER BLACK. SNAGSNAKE
CLOUDS !
Strata of dawn fires et hrahh gray gwor blur hrooo.
GRAHH GRAH GROOOR DANN HEER.
Cloud down bed volcano peak. Sharks' backs
swimming in eternity tooo ! THOU ! TOW !
LOVELY LADY CITY ME.
Lake of floating islands, blue lights, grass, new ayre.
GRAHAYORR !

(landing in Mex City — morn)

OOOOH. HOHH! OOH. HRAHH ME GO TORR
back bye ne bee. Hrr. Gruh grahh neegoww
hrahh bweeze mahtote bweee hrahhr,
hrahhrr,
so sad and different love I weep here for you noh
I cool m'brahh me where you noh city is a treasure
or a woman spryahh whann thoo sa ieee
slaff dim. NOH! FORBIDDEN FALSEHOOD!
SAD UNTRUTH!
TRULY I DO NOT CRY NOR FEEL —
but so far inside is a whirlwind I ride.
OH!
OH!
OH!
WHY AM I HERE?
LEEOOOOO ME WEEP — TRULY . . .
No mantra, no tantra, no poetry . . .
NOH TEEERZ.

(Mex City — eve)

HROHH MARR ! MARR ! GAHROOH ! YAIEER !
The hand dripping blood floats in the air. Roses. Hallways.
Doors.
I have discovered silence. This is real !
THOU
separate one. Thou difference. Thou every sole warm thing.
THOU HRAHRRG ! THOU GREEEARR ! THOU
SNEL !
Married to me grahhr and heeeer. NAH-NOH !
NAH-NOH ! Heeer and grahhr me to married !
Separate one. Thou difference. Thou every sole warm thing.
THOU
I have discovered silence this is real !
The hand dripping blood floats in the air. Roses. Hallways.
Doors.
HROHH MARR ! MARRR ! GAHROOh ! YAIEER !
YAHHR ! HAND. ME !

(San Francisco)

Alpha and Omega tunnel to still energy grahh-tha
Thou me met to still grey thahhr thoon.
THRAHHR THONETT GRAHH
ROO-OOOOOOOO-OOOOOOOOO-OOOOOR !
Place wings upon words and rohrs.
Grahhgrool gahrooo wipps mahoove.
OOH NOH THOW MEE TOH TORNY
seeking
eternity
THOU-ME
THOW!
!GAHROOOOOOOOOOH!

NOH VISION I WANT BUT THE FLESH
OF ME BRINGING THEE-THOU
tooorm now bye-tha being two loves together mrahh
of our grooh thowmm narg froooo byme
NAKRAYOTHBAHKTA GRITOOORM BLIST.
MOORBWAH ! TOWM !
Woman holding a child who is a woman
holding a child. GREE HANT
shawl of holding el coolorrs.
Thy in and about brooo nah mooom
bweeth. Mahkeeng oon eer gant. SEE !
Woman holding a child who is a wooman
holding gree-hant a child.
THHAHHRNOOM GRAHHHHH.
Modest. Modest. Modest holding a suckling.
THY BABE.

GROWLL-PRAYSE-GROOOR MEBETH THOOON !
SHY-TORR BRAUN FEEL THOW NOH PEN
me-orr grabrek teth troon sru trrrr.
OHH OHHH OH FOOL GOOD
sweeeeze me noth brythek-toorn be nohh blekkarr.
HOOO-OOOOOOOO-OOOOL HROHH !
GRAH ! GRAH ! GRAHH ! GREEER ! NORT
aiiee swed nort by noth tone be lonet.
Moth-dappled scent of fullness, winged light
in the passage by thahrrnow bet
back be a candle too thar bahd
ool things in thee strem hoh-ooh now.
THOH !
You are here this is my body groor.

ROOOR ! MAHROOOR ! GAHARR ! NARGHHR !
STAHR MEET STARR NAHG-NAR !
BRAHOOOOOOOO ! BRRAHOOOO-
OOIEE !

Thow art mee now thoot leeve kahrnak trar noorwybe !

BEGROOAOAR ! BEGRAYOOOAIEER !

Roo grahaahr nar thapp grow-weett snoowie
gondlapp make beet torny. Mahweeb mahweeb tha loot
bween.

OOOH-AH ME AH OOH NOOR THEE LITE

me my me noor ! Mahroor gaharr ! Narghhr !

The uselessness ! The lung ! The purpose
is a hand, a love, a groan, a tear.

A SMILE.

A grahh, a graharr, a . . .

SNAHRR OOH WEE MEET LAHV !

When I am tired my eyes press hard — I blink. Rahhr
and ahn cam groos thee oww nite meer nite
in calm thou rage noh but theee stillness in
ENERGY WITE. WHOLE, WE ARE ALL
whole, there is a transcendent beauty rising from underneath
the graohhr and roohoor to breeth nowt-ooh.
BWOOOH ! AHN ! BWOOOOH NAHK.
WE
ARE
MODEST
CREATURES
waiting ooh be gahoosed be mild eeeze.
Be thou here away now there.

CHAIRS DRAPED IN WHITE TERRYCLOTH.
PALM-FERNS SPRAY TO THE CEILING.
Light of gahoor grahh narr, completion of hrahhrr,
mist of evening in dree mahhr. OOH-NAH HOOR.
Mrahh grooor drooped nooh ah thoorn jahnrah.
YOU, I LOVE ALL THINGS, YOU
twist of space coiled in me and outer thah you.
Heer be back by thoon me-tath-norr. These my
experiments to give ease to the future.
Goorblesh thee mahthoon torntoor bythnapp
dark wood and violet bynoth toorsh roohrr.
Stillness, stillness whisper thy greeahoor
UV.
DOOOHNIEEE !

THY NOOHR ! THY OOOGRESHK ! THOU PLAID
LITE
THOU THOWW ! TOOOM-KREER MAK-EEZE
by thou bleem swarr-ret-nok-thah ooh-ahr snoo wahr
port mak-eeze belshthep shaboth-taktar breen in heer by me.
GRAHH GAHROOOOOR,
GAHROOOOOOOOOOOOO.
Greeeer gyreeahhr bemayoth nahhr grahharr hrahhr.
Noh blemish narr but a perfect beauty als neer
graybraeoth pemeter nahhr I theeayow kall
to thy order, me thou leet tabreez nahtoon shayboth —
! OH !

OH ! NAH OOH ! — EHH ! GRAHHR-ROOH !
KAHR MEEST ROOOHR, BYE THA MEE NORR
OOH WEET MEE TEV VOOON NAHHR.
By thy boolt me thah heer mee bye thoon grahn
heer nohth bwah heer nothak beenoor bythe nekk.
Heer gahroor neth grahooor thooon bleth bye neth
oooooh noh toor thee ah oon
write by my breth on a silver scrool
and cast it into thyne grahoor grahahr por mahh
thy doon stahr zaybooth mak-lee nohr.
NOH ! NOH ! NOH ! HOOOOR !
Ooblesh my. Bahhr tha groooh ?
HEEEEER !
SHARRAH ! SHREEEIIEE ! SRAHHH !

THE PINE CONE IS PERFECT, IT STANDS BY
THE FOOT OF THE MAIDEN.
No, it is upon the table. The furniture is grahoor. The light is
gahrhoor.
This is in bliss eternity. Oh calm gahrr groooh nahrr
la ahhr NOOOHH ! Marr sum vahhr grahrraiee hrahhr
nok-thorp naharr. No rise up ! No stand out !
BUT STEADY !
STEADY ! STEADY
as she goes.
I am thy-my flagged flesh ship.
GRUHH. NOOOOH ! HAHHR ! BLOOW !
Bluhh
!

BLERM ROOM, I LOVE YOU, CARRY ME
WITH YOU —
bynor groom. Noktathorr rahhr shu graharr
beem loov grayhowr empty empty full wretchedness
becoming joy love cone by lite of heer noooh
reem 'ptah; grooh gaharr goooor grah be emmeeii
THRAH ! NOH ! BWEM ! MORNOO !
THEE ME.
THOU I.
Us heart roar twain oons.
Bhwei !
Shapeful shapeliness noh space sounds droor.
Chair like a darkly varnished butterfly.
Hillside cascade of clear water.
Orange vines. Mattress & velvet.
Solo candle.
Beloved weirdnesses
escaped from thy boy's mind.

NORRTHOW ! OOOHMEE ! NOG LITE ! NOO
dorr kann bee blayke leet eer noo tow thownie
dann brekk thay mah torr blust noh breshk bakk
mag me toww noh oww thoonie meeee blest !
KHRAHRR ! SHELF ! TEEMOWW !
Teem now oodorr sen bless I thee ooh-nohh
carnal air of wax portrayed in smoke.
THEE OWW OHH MY
sung & sad fabled sleeping self
grahoored to waking gowwr.

Huge shadow shades of gray violet and air bwoooh upp
slant sleeping rahoon. Droor grahagrr dooooor
me thype ahhrg thin ayre bwuhh shroooh shriee.
SANTOR ! NAKK ! BEWL ! PRESHK !
No empty here thow me I sorn.
GOOOOOOOOOOOOOOR !
GRAHOOOOOOOOOOOR !
NOHH ! AH NO!
But ooohbleshk tha noor tha groor
drooping rise.

OH AIR, THOU POISON, ENABLER OF PHEN-
OMENALITY. LET ME DRINK SPIRIT
AND SPATTER
LAUGHTER !
But no strain grahhr beth noh blayne komm
hrock ten deeeth nye ahh ohh lowve eeeeeze imm nee
doork. Tow thoraynie klarr kran moohbeeeze.
OH NEVER ARE WE MISTAKEN
in ahhr grarrhr nooh,
graharr noooh, grahhhr nooh.
DEEN !
Rooooooooooooooooooh ! !

THRAHHRRR ! GRAHAHHR ! NORR GRAHH ! !
GAHHR
nooh leet ! Shrahhr sweeeeze darg geeyeaor an tha noob
queayr mah bleshtorr ooze weeelt tabnoh ehh nah booty.
AHNK HONN LESH FELL TOOH ZEE KAY
and garr experience is a dreeft of the willed experience
in your brain hayre moovie being
BUT
REAL.
Tha hooor tha kraan, tha scrool-dev-neese.
Beeaytorr nath tohk bel seen melt in thee ahh eeze.
ASSERT THYE NAH AND YAYY THOH !

OH THOU LAMP, CHAIR, SUGAR, DRUNKNESS
seen by calm ahn grooing reahoar. Noor heaorr gahhr —
HRAHH ! SHREEAIIEE ! AH THOOH LEAVE
meh ahh-ooh-bresh tean. Ehn eenk rise ahn zahvorr
oh-feer-ayne, tah meehle snord lite fayze driff horr.
THOOON ! THOOON ! GRAHAORR !
Through the char ahh noh-eeh Koarahs and winged
Doric pleasure in the reservoir of still silence.

— — — — — — — — — — — — — — — — — — — —

OH NOHH !

— — — — — — — — — — — — — — — — — — — —

but oh, oh ever.
Heer en nah thooh. Thy oooblesh uhn frah weeb gahrr heen.
Me thah rahrings ! !
ETT NOOOH !
NOOH NAHYARR ! Dreeeze.

Russet and manzanilla, hot water steaming, pink and red
noharrs,
bleezeleets, rohr mantras, gruumblings, black circles
with eagle's pinions, tides of eyes and noses —
WE HEER MOVE IN TA
EN I OH NAH OH KAH THY NOOHARR —
boot me nuhh ah zolleed pemeter krohss eem foohl oh ahh ness
sah eeh shayabayoth. Groor brayze nul la
oose nah wheet in roose nolt em-brektoth
krann nor dee teii oayhh-oh thow kernak borteen.
By thah blek nee bee thorn too thouww THOW !
TOO THOUWW *THOW*
TOO THOUWW *THOW*!
Meeeeeeeeeeeeeen dra!

Bah nee thell oh toor mahk graah by owhr note whee
del nohr thape, sahr zahr noth be blite en oohr coop ya.
Soong bleeze byle. Breet-toe-skane weel mahg
ayhne skhrahn toolh-orr-nye blesh toh mahr.
MAHR-GAHROOOOOOOOOOOO ! Doe neth by auk
thee senate aug beeese. Hoohl ehn grarr grahh.
BEL NECK TAH TORR. OOOOH SWEEEZE !
By ooh bleesh mah loove thee im russle thee ah may
by bee-norr kem dahze seelv keen beh noohl
— UHH ! SEEEZE MAYNAH !
Ash me noh toor frahn moh tooh napp bee brekk
tee orr my dool krann swez-tel-thak shabathoh
im essem dahze makk lahvoon. Ta doonoor,
that ooblesh kander foor tahtoon ehn
eel-ekk sweeze born to be makk seelnabatt, ohf snorr

NA TORRNA.

MARILYN MONROE, TODAY THOU HAST PASSED
THE DARK BARRIER
— diving in a swirl of golden hair.
I hope you have entered a sacred paradise for full
warm bodies, full lips, full hips, and laughing eyes !
AHH GHROOOR. ROOOHR. NOH THAT OHH !
OOOH . . .
Farewell perfect mammal.
Fare thee well from thy silken couch and dark day !
AHH GRHHROOOR ! AHH ROOOOH. GARR
nah ooth eeze farewell. Moor droon fahra rahoor
rahoor, rahoor. Thee ahh-oh oh thahrr
noh grooh rahhr.

(August 6, 1962)

HAHHR ROH NORR THAR RAH GRAHG
ahh thee doohr. Ah wee no thap kran moor
coffee, the fogs arise, drift, frah, nooh too oh
broo noor grahh. Nooh weep be my skroll thah
thy oh neen ooh marr dahoww tha neet
drips teerz ah me zahd. Thee, oh, my Dahoor
breth. AIEOOO AIEEEE YEEORR
GRAHHH ! !
RAGOOOR ! GARR ! GRAHHH . . .
Blissfulness hidden by no veils and not there.
But here, ragooooor, oh my bleesh.
THAH OHH OOOH ME
my ooh mee ole tree meed.

Sweeeeze noh bleeethe ahn groor nah deiize
troog ghrarr garr rooh krann eh-no-ohbleesh
sweetness of grey heer to back nort bah thahnn
sweeld drome naza oorgasteth tookromm bektor.
Thou singing science of being silence im rahoor.
Oh honeyed singer when the body is a brain
of physiology,
gah rahooling grhahn thy cooning
skool aye nrah gross nah toones.
Oooh shweeze ooh thah noh I oh
dreer nah krye grool. Toosk na ooony
yahl then brohtony im sweelze, im hoorny,
for toh.
NO-MORE-HEART

NO MORE HEART POR AH GROOHNIE
bood schleeze. Oooh waz mhee tharr im bresh.
Ooh was poor imbresh.
NHARR ! DRINK THY INTOXICATED SKULL
to being from the cup of lovingness ! — We are !
WE ARE ! WE ARE ! THERE IS
a radiant chorus
and a lyre of poor man's rahhrs
of immortality in every thought and gesture.
Drunken on the full vase of emptiness
and proudly vahrm en grooing
to eh oh thah
tah gloods ehn trah hooor im
thah kroonie oold — hoohv ess.
— Mhoogsh fhwoooh ! —

HOOR THA HOOOREEZE NOKROMETH RAHHR
thah deem oh breee mee oonlite *nooorr.*
Brahoon. Marr, eee lahnn ooth dormeth kine theee
— *aiie!* Ayohh ! Bresh ! Thoon im leeve roosell
why will be we dream to more thahn we are?
Sreeeee ! Bahm thipt, plip-plop, drook koord.
Grahh gaharr grooo. Wheeze dool rahoor
uv fawcets. Infants of all warmths sleep cuddling
in the grey universe. Ten trillion billion curled
and being babes each dear to their
encircled and unacted beings . . . Countless
innocent eyes and fresh senses,
and none with doubt or question.
And we of good sense grow outward —
oohr wahh — from those kinder.
We ever be that way. The bloodlust of the weasel cub
eese brite ahn hahh looveeh !

The stargleam in the white translucent cup
and sienna depth below. The blue, green and pale purple
light upon the white eeze ah oh pit weet hahn
thy hoor im mee I ahh noor say tha hee !
THOU PERFECT MATERIAL FOREST
I move and breathe within.
NOOR RAHH HARR NOH MAHDEER.
I listen to thee
and hear
night flowers
and doubt thy, my, every, permanence
so happily.
— Each spoon a mantra !

PALE BLUE UPON GLEAMING WHITE
and perfumed smoke
groon stirp oooh ah reeze owp thowrr
nah-oh kontach heer me ahthoo thy hidden
niches, particles, corners, doorways, cornices,
and interstices ahh breeing mohoars
ahn thah hooh grahhr stay
be mah-hoo. Nah tah thornakk
jahn orm bleesh.
NAH ! AHH-AOHH AIEEE NAH-NOH !
Karnak bray breeoth deel cortay
la ayohh eeem food frah thahh deepze.
THE HUGE HIGH SILENCES,
THE HUGE LOW SILENCES,
the silences ahv gahhr.
— The thumb.
The deepth grahhze ehs empty noor.

IN THE GRAY BLACK SILENCE THE RADIANCE
PIERCES THE TASSELS
and the night shows through. Here. Now. Everywhere.
Where I look. And I am seeing thoohh.
GOOOOOR RAHH! GRAHH! NOWTH
DROON DOOOOOOOOR AHG!
Nardroor yeyb now thowtak drahrr ooh me thet noh
large faint rain dreeps oopon the frale tha toor
glooing gaharr ayaiieooo. Moh hee jine im buhorr.
Tartak thownee zeshabayoth-otoor scrooon
in the heer ahn nooh farr hi aygleh mountains.
The breeze.
The tassels.

KRYBESH LHARR KROARMETT OOOH AH NEE
too thowwr meebresh skann nahdeeeer braeyiou.
Drohhr brekk skrool muhn gah leet gahrooh
rahhr; drooom kraydresh zwee veeorr ghhrayhoar.
DROOOM AHH ME NORTH TI SVOON
han thee moood droom
eeze mah aeyoww.
Nacht thahrr in eeze ett doom byorr blud
por dee tha kay YAIEEE! Grahaorr !
GARR ! GARRR ! GREEE
aeiiooop tathoon een ez beeeze nath thoose
en ell oak leeves bah theee baz
HEEEEEER GAORRRRRRR BE !
Ahhh-oooooooh. Norrrrrrrrr . . .

REEEZE AH TOWW OOOH THAH HEEN
shao sharrrr dreeth garr neeth breeze ahm veee
tah heeer, tha ooom leed pyorr drowth em lay hahz
NOOOOOOOR! NOOOOOOOR! NOOOOR
in the full noon that deeh est ahhum graype
fahr dah-thorreept vaysse wharr oooh norrr
thownie heer. In the roolings rahaorr grooh
cahsparr er ez noor whar thy voices eternally
raise us tho ta puzzlement solidly in grahh.
HERE! HERE! HERE!! OH!
Oh, the ragged blossoms kann grahrr theese.
Here. Here. Here. Oh!
TARRRRARR! GRAHOOOOL.

SILENCE THE EYES ! BECALM THE SENSES !
Drive drooor from the fresh repugnance, thou whole,
thou feeling creature. Live not for others but affect thyself
from thy enhanced interior — believing what thou carry.
Thy trillionic multitude of grahh, vhooshes, and silences.
Oh you are heavier and dimmer than you knew
and more solid and full of pleasure.
Grahhr! Grahhhr! Ghrahhhrrr ! Ghrahhr. Grahhrrr.
Grahhrr-grahhhhrr ! Grahhr. Gahrahhrr Ghrahhhrrrr.
Ghrarrrr. Ghrahhr ! Ghrarrrr. Gharrrr. Ghrahhhrr.
Ghrahhrr. Ghrahr. Grahhr. Grahharrr. Grahhrr.
Grahhhhr. Grahhhr. Gahar. Ghrahhr. Grahhr. Grahhr.
Ghrahhr. Grahhhr. Grahhr. Gratharrr ! Grahhr.
Ghrahrr. Ghraaaaaaahrr. Grhar. Ghhrarrr ! Grahhrr.
Ghrahrr. Gharr ! Ghrahhhhr. Grahhrr. Ghraherrr.

Gahr thy rooh gaharr eeem thah noolt eeeze
be me aiee grahorr im lowvell thee thy lips and hair
are stunning field byorr ayohh mah ahn teerz.
Ghroo ahn the green-blahk trees
are tall ahn brooding in the dark gray-pink
wet mist of night. All is flashes of silver
upon damp black by scroolt in theer.
THEE,
THEE,
THEE
mahk flooors pore reeer, thah noose eem rakd.
GAHARRRRR GAYRR RRAH MEEN LOOVEEE.
And all physicality is poesy
to demanding flesh.

Ring tailed cat.
Close Arcturus.
Heavenly visions of gentle rats with pink noses.

I LOVE TO THINK OF THE RED PURPLE ROSE
IN THE DARKNESS COOLED BY THE NIGHT.
We are served by machines making satins
of sounds.
Each blot of sound is a bud or a stahr.
Body eats bouquets of the ear's vista.
Gahhhrrr boody eers noze eyes deem thou.
NOH. NAH-OHH
hrooor. VOOOR-NAH ! GAHROOOOO ME.
Nah droooooh seerch. NAH THEE !
The machines are too dull when we
are lion-poems that move & breathe.
WHAN WE GROOOOOOOOOOOOOOOR
hann dree myketoth sharoo sreee thah noh deeeeeemed ez.
Whan eeeethoooze hrohh.

WHAHN WE NROH HEEER AHN THEE
thah thow me. Deep stoch roohr im furnooze meat
ahn grahooor een seelanze viola sreee shareeeee.
AH THEE LOVE TOW THOU
oor roon dreep hor note ah me myorr.
Plahn. Plahn. Thooreeee dooorthone.
Pluhn. Plunh. Thooreeeeeeee nrosh tooo
oor tow. Thri thrash hah ! Meeebresh mebreth hyaii.
Ooothoon droobresh metheeee. Here
down deep-over and above
thy heart's ache !
Plahn. Plahn drooooo. Dowr mrethreeeee.
Where the unspoken voice speaks before the teerze dreep.
Thy message my be.

(written during
Schubert's Amadeus Quartet)

THIS IS MY BODY'S WORK. MY MIND IS HE
noor thahln ahh deem err. Droor moveth . . . Aeiiiiiiii
naieee ayeii hrahh voh dann wheeesh tonn thoor moobesh
hoh well drann srii weshtoth moshyboth toureee —
drann thy touress. Rohh hyeee gahRAHHRR
sweesly. Wheeyoh ohn ell brezeth porbresh droon.
Broon ah labronteth por esh el moobwath-HAH.
GAHRAH POOOR ER ES TOOH AYY THOWNEY.
Mah taharoooneii wellstove. Selahh toh nah thoney
wheeer es meesheeress tyeeeth moh eratony —
WHAHH DROOHN THE LAKE
reflecting beauties
of multitudinous holy sweetlings
tumt harungggggggggggggggggggggg

(Amadeus Quartet)

The motion of cool air shudders my shoulders with pleasure.
The smoke from nostrils makes flame-shaped wings.
The air is soft.
AYE.
The air is soft and smooth.
Aye! Aye!
ROOHGRAHOOOOOOOOOOR-
DEEEEEP-AYE-GRAH
rahagraooor. Grahh. Garrr grahoor hrahhrr
miketoobrometh-por-eshkry. Rahoooor gahhr. Narl
opal, nahr sorottbreth. Drooon-dep karnoh pohr ell
and deeper deeper to the feeling being
to the risen-acting dream cave
walking & talking.
HERE, AYE, HERE.
AYE. AYE.
Up-deep. Aye ! Thou I thou thoooh.

OHGREEOSH NAHTOOHR GRAHNDU THOHMM
byoor krohnee nakgreebresh — bwohh thahlltoom.
Behind I leave thee in my soaring.
Roooshoobwooeth gruhn kooolnakturnie.
August. Summer. Air.
Rooh ordaineth hrukk groosharneth dahhn
oohr eeeze nak-tree-ohbreshk. Leaf flocks
in clusters gathering
for their flight.
Sheep, rabbits, sharks — awake or dreaming.
The seasons are plushy banners of Maya
waving about me where I stand.
And I ah oohh I am solid velvet.
VALVOOH DROOOOH HYAH.
OHGREEEOSH NAHTOOHR GRAHNDU THOHMM.

OHGREEOOO DAKTURNY VIOLET NAH THOOON
theh drahmur, teh breshmooder, thy oh tha,
belltreeeoort nak-teeort ohbryesh thah needing
thy pleasing face in profile crossed by radiant stripes
of love, thy hands and hips mohrlak droon
seeray nooorapp. All sounds are unjudgemented love to thee.
OH GREEOOVDAKTURNY VIOLET NAH THOOON.
Theh drahmur, teh breshmooder, thy oh tha,
thy pleasing face in profile crossed by radiant stripes
of love, thy hands and hips mohrlak droon.
Seeray noorapp all sounds are unjudgemented love to thee.
AHSZHOOOR ! DROOOM !
Brek
me
tort.

Leed mohgruhhr imm halooh the speed & the motion pass
and I am totally left — not suffering.
Bruhh hoohl zallay always. Hrohhh gahreeeh hrahh
ghrahrr gahroooh. Ooohr noh teetapp
GHRAHH, GAHRR, GARRR
em leeve lowve. Law thy healds.
Warmed, warmed, marmed noh, nor ought konned
by yeelering edistry pharms. DROOOOO-
HOOOOOOOR GHRAHH
gahrow hrahhr yah. Ooodrometh.
Drimmed bood ahreeezayne.
Flahn aback aber ztroong.

THE DARK BLUE SNAKE FLARES UP FROM THE LOINS
and lashes itself upon the mukti'd air
writhing the clouds of unspoken speeches
and making fragrance of hemlock & copal.
I see the lovers seated in groups upon the hillside;
they converse
in heroic whispers ahv ghroar ahnd torreze
reading their fates upon the scrolls whose bare arms
unroll them for the dimmed
but bare and staring eye. — In the garden
we are beyond such nonsense and we smile.
OOOH HAH TATHONEY
MEEEEREBB NOH OOHGRIER.
Grooohrr manes uncurl from our cheeks
and we know it. Thah Oh.

Lha drey mi chew-nang chig. Over the veil it is same
as before — infinitely, infinitely. Krama drah goor.
Keemyab bruhm. Inifitely, infinitely and always
perfect music, oh listener.
KRAH NA YAH GROOAHOAOOOOOOO SARIII
SOOOOOOOOOOOOOOOOEEEEESE.
Ya ! Aieee yahroohar. It is how deep that we
make it,
hearing its feel, watching the lightning in the dark gleaming
purple blue.
OOOOOH AYAHOAYY THEE !
OOAYHOHH !
And other shimmering real fakes.

SHAGA SHE NOWRTHOOM BYRE NEEKROP
OOOH EZ ATHAH THEEOWNY
thoww-looze. Oooh ez athar toww oh brisgkerr
grahgoor garr hrg-garr rooor nragroor rahh.
GRAHH! GRAHH! GHRAHHAEII
ROWWRRR . . .
Sharnagyam — grayaii oohbresh . . .
THOWW-OUTOONIE. *TOWW!*
Roooombrathakasheel brathaaaa . . .
AAIEEOU.

GRAHGRAYOOOR BLANG. BLANG-GROOOOOR
sharnagtreii greee say-oornake dann thay siteee got,
thy dooombreethe ooh ah toww, toww. Ooh ezz ayee.
Oh I call for thee to rise out of me . . .
But no need, no need, thy fleshwarm
and technicolor, sleep sleek, sweet smelling,
breasted soft thighed pleasance, more than more
abound thah noohr rhoon oogweshk loooh vye
thou, thow yeer drahooeth, grahrrgooo. Rooosh
oosweed softer thah noh ah hoor seeted thah
steeped nah oh hooreeze rydeen.

I have changed again; I am somebody else who is more
like me.
GRAAGHHR MOOOZSH-THAYRE HAIERAH.
Lonely, stilled, filled, calm and full of energy.
Let thy pleasure rise. Oh how I long grahooor
nak aghh braie-hooor gragrayne thy nooorzshe nah
hayy oooh my deem bledd kamm toww dooorndreth.
SHAYMEAKTOR GROOOHH !
OHH AHH LEVE THAH BROOSTS
DOKEENEE TAH NOOORBRETH
buds & petals
through all the nights.

OH THOU FARTHER AWAY THAN HEAVEN,
APPEAR FOR I MISS THEE,
I long
in the gloom foggy noon for thy intentness.
The blue-black & gleaming blot of spirit drips
upon the chalk white wall
and makes your features, ears, & smile.
GRAYOHH GREYGRAHARR YEO YI-EEE
DEELOMY. Silver stick, red candle
and blue yellow flame.
HAHNOOOOOR HRAHRR METHONY
GARRR GRAHHH NAY-AIEOOOOO
NARR.

HRAGREEOH GROANOOOR DAM-THYBEKK
my own reflection flaring and shimmering
in the blackened window
— LET IT FADE TO REAL SOLIDITY !
AH NAHH NAH NOOOR,
torments give way to enlightened pleasure !
THEE OH, eeh ahh ay-ohwahn. Meh ahh gnooor.
Oh I am lonely, lonely, lonely till ezz
ohl hooors meh. EHH AHH OHH . . .
YEHRAYZSHTROTH !
SHABREOSHTRANTHOR !
Nay,
ever-echoing trumpet of physicality.
I seek the secret ever-billowing steadier.

RAHGRAYHOOOM DRAHHOOOR
eeen esh tell drorhzy. Oh mee horm tow !
Oooh mee hahaow oorm chezz in the night,
in vast tiny cup drink flowers. Thee, thou, oh
thy ears and missing laughter. Razeeer nah
gratoom kalyx. Oh, OH, OH, OH, thah hayiee !
The silence fleets away and with it
thy return ! So I raise myself
to drink the stillness.
Cloud miracle creature nah dreen
TOOOORR NAK OWBREEOSH
THY QUAVERINGS,
THY NOW HERE EVER !

Blue pot and dripping water, lighted circle, pearl pink flame,
and smoke. The elf blood rises in our veins and whispers
— we are strange and deep
unknown creatures of unspoken melodies :
GRAYHAYYOWW REEEEEER WEEE GRAHH.
— OOOH NAYY TAYOWW WEEEEB, OOOH
THAH. OOOOOH GRAHHH RAYHOOAYORR
RAHHR ROOOOW MAH TAY OHWNEY TEEERZ.
GRAHOOOOOOOOOOR AIEEHOWW RAHTOOHR
TAE AYOH-MAH. RAYHOWW MAH TREEEZE
OOOHRR GRAHH GAHHHHR.
OOOOOOOOOOOO-
OOOOOOOOH …
Dreening trah ahtooor nez-rooooh …

((PALE PEARL PINK ON THE WALLS
AND OUR DAYDREAMS
projected outward in solid reality.
We hear, we touch, we breathe. Partitions rustle
and we do not care among the creakings and thumps
nah gayothorrs for we are incarnate joys.
ROGTRAYOMF! ROGTRAYOMF!
Each nostril is a booming perfection.
The blackened skulls and rusty bolts
are only a background
for
meat
warmth
that passes to something more.

I like your eyes Liberty!

Steam drips the windows in front of utter darkness
that's so deep it's cool and sweet. Forget it.
Take more wings love.))

((ROGREEOSH, FOR I HAVE DREAMED
of thee forever. Reeehosh it is
AN INSTANT !
Forget, forget, for the Universe is in a state
of triumph. We have arisen with it !
We climb with twining figures
to multitudinous heavens that are all here
where we're singing. It does not matter,
it does not matter, joyous glorious garhoosh
grayhayarhoooosh nargrowm thayolesh
tathor myobeth where we throw
the spot light of our souls . . .
Thy eyed feet and thy scented ribbon's passage
among the bloomings !))

((OOOOGREEEOSH-DRATHOR BUTTERFLY
BEATS AND PANTS DRATHOOOOR ABOUT
THE GROWING RING OF PANSIES
where the earth is dry garhroon nahh dree-
opeth barhoooth nohdresh beethorr noh
I oh thah meeerdown emrah gahrsoon.
Oooomreeeoh ahn drahgnooze. Theeeow !
Water seeps within the earth
between the roots.
The bee faints with bliss of overwork
and curls her leg.
Snail hunger fills the air with rasping teeth
thrown out from the cave beneath the leaf.
Ooor ahm geahzthow fon kalein.
Wah lahg dooohr ohgreeeazsh shtahr.))

RAHOOOOOOR GRAHH GRAHOOOOOOO,
still peace where art thou? I me ahrrn garr
thah booon enn ez sweeeort here. Wah dreen emm ez dooth.
Appear and please me as thou half appearest :
red pen, yellow brush, black lamp.
NOWERHOWWROWW ! GREEEORRT ! !
Morning is a dolorous crimson.
I hear thy mocha azz oon kloor !
The leaves are quiet as the stilled pains of all beings
quann ooh reshtor. Aseeg tah
breshkly weeekly and here thou art.
Nod we things toww !
Thah rearing rahgroosh nothing.
Tiger cowrie shell-dappled brown and rust.
Turquoise locks shaking on the faces
of men and their daughters.
Rasheeeoh-ootrohh.

I've made it ! Here is total acceptance and god-belief
wrapped in one hagreeow graharr
en nooth tase tah bleem howshee-ortow ladder
of souls em tatlool schvarz enn nooh dohr
nag abroon ein graz nothing !
HAYY ! AIE ! YRAHHROOOO ! YARR ! HREI !
DRINK
AND
COME
AND
DRINK WITH ME !
Step over into thah eempty Shrahh . . .
BROOOOOOSH MOWR !
HAGREOSHPETHTORR !

— — — — — — — — — —

Here in the fine heat and degrees in plashtor.
FROWW !

GARR GROWW MARRRRR THAHROOOOOOH
zynooort kam theyohh em koold wand thy hustlings
from deepness thah groort reezen owp voordz
emm mah tayohh NAH ! HO,
GRAHZNOOOR GRAHH GHARAHH GROARR
speeding en coolness oh feel I that heereeze
and the doom lite we devour
swinging grahharr out from futility to praise,
passing the easy information
in the City of Nothing
where there are roses again and moist dahlias
of touch and sound calling to you.
Typewriters of mystery and ferns
ett aye-oh lah. The grim gray becoming what we
once knew and have forgotten.
THE VOICE THAT IS ETERNAL.

THE STARS ARE A SHIELD OF NOTHING
CREATED OF NOTHING
AND I CALL ON THEE TO SWING,
ashahh harr marrr gahrooo yahr aye-howw tanthor rahrr
ooohrnah thownie toww smeels tor sheen
thah gahreems wooven mah laughter eehn nroh
beyond the final first devi now shemetter
poor ahn gras nowerhoww hayrayoar
bleth tomakayne grahhr shageer
raise up thy heeze ahn streee entoh eeze.
LOOK UP !
See our calm, titanic, minuscule gestures.
YAHRR NOH. HRAHHHRR-NOHH !

ROWWSHNEEOWR THRRAHRR GREEEEOOO
eem bleeethe noose yeeort. The marble
of streaked scarlet and black is soft as a lamb.
Troon agah yayythowwr teen freeng
in the mist among trahz broooohr trees
and all breetenth whann thee man-jerr
singing ahn droosch enn couples. THEE !
OH THEE ! THAH BLEEESCH NOOR !
Walking amidst them and weeping in chorus
of joy.
I heernarr.

HAGREOHSHAPTOR THE SUNSHINE DU VARM
een ess eeltah fahh thah noooerowty grahntoor
GARRH GREEEAHR GROOOOOOR THAMEEZE
ahh eeze noohrbahh. Ah bleesh
heeze shooogahh thah dowmy trooolt meorr
yaye tharoom bee loovah seeeek nahhr
ooohbreeorohtesh. Ooooh thou! Frahm grah
by thee aye-ohh avrah feengereeng schoonblowth.
The faces peer down smiling as if thahnghroo
light were not material
ahn thee grooozree owf frahn dezmeeer ! Shemmehstra !

The leaves shine green-brown covered with sweet sap
and we remember the warmth arising
to meet warmth
in drashoooh spreed rays tathoor oww nahrr
in drathoohr shrooomm troosh allbeg-renny danshoor
bloosh regahn voohr schrool dan roosh may-tort may lapp
zeeeoww tyne blahr. Aye. Nay. Hrayohh. Tine. Thash !
OH TAH RAYSHEEAH-MEEOWP TOOR !
Ah, gentle daily recurring Spring tah weer mettrah !
I cannot smell thee, I cannot smell thee
for my senses dim with thah rahooreeling tides
nah salee-osh breeeeetohhrr ! Hhnn.

HROWSHNAHTOOORNY KAMBLEKK TYETORR
ooh thah krahhrn eem esh ahgk nah toosh shprek.
The flying spots upon the air ahn froon kibersch nofbooord.
NOH ! OGREOSH !
oh, OOOH, dimpled reality, I thee seek, thy
mensorium owgth ahn thah thowwerett.
OH, YES, HERE ARE THE WARM TORSOS
COILED IN THE NESTS
OF IMMEDIATE CHANGING GROOOHRAHH.
Nygethowp roooohoosheowsh, lah ween roozle.
Emm esh shooolahh dowwr.
The benign eyes stare in from outside droomah.

Oh thah oorn dreen nah blemish ultimo.

Wrinkles of cracked smiles upon all matter beaming anew
with tah floosh nah greaaagattor
— I HAVE SEEN THEE !
AND I DON'T CARE ! I DON'T !
On the piano I played an ultimate chord.
It started bright ivory yellow and swiftly
turned to black
and I left it hanging forever . . .
till I put my fingers to the keys again.
AHN DENN YOH SHOR TAH ME GROW THAH
TOOR NHROHH GROBESHK. TAHN-TOOOOOR
KROSHOMETH KEW KNEW THA HOOOR
HERE THY TOOMESH TROOOM IM —
OH ! YAH ! HOH YASH . . .
Warm furry beasts curled in caves
SPEEERESH DROOOSHKESS DREEEZ !

AH WEEEEBD WOOORDS THAH NOOR ARRHMS
EEEH GROOOL TAH KEEERT ESSING
VOOOH MAH SWEEEZE.
Reeezen til ahn trooort tah nort flooon
what tah vass seelhoooeeen drooomt og days.
The beings are so strange. Smiles leave trails.
Ahh the soohree kal sheep nohr tess leebnoh
ahn ahr wave-beat grakeen.
Oh thou mysterious steps into black everywhere
and the eyes of nothing
watching us
while the wet soul waves form gentle faces
above the howling.
I see the human figures as I pass.
We grahrgroo mag oohr mahr tan hoopfal melodien.

Nahg treee towm heeer een hahhr grahzeeng
thah een mah hoohrt nra droor thah ess me.
OOOHN OOHRT SWELTESS!
Thahn breeze ahn hallways again. Thah chairs,
enmeorr darkness tablets. Ah hoon reezen.
I here now go nowhere
memoring and calling thy soft hair.
Oh doohrm thah nog towhown esseee tah blyme,
all flowing out me creating of my seen thou.
We fly from the truth swollen with benign tortures
hallucinating the real image of pleasure . . .
NAH! NOH! NOH! HRAHHH . . . !
Nah aye mee-oong rang troon een loodahm.
All creatures of sweetness in ascent
like waverings of air . . .
Toes, eyes, lungs & lobes regneen ahn metter
and purposefully willfully wavering in the now.
Grooooooooooooooooooooooor!!
GROOOOOOOOOR! GRAHHH! HARR!
Meeowp nar.

Grah gooooor ! Ghahh ! Graaarr ! Greeeeeeer ! Grayowhr !
Greeeee
thah noort em bleethe ! Hroooom garayowth gahhr !
In the dim lowered senses enn ess ell warmth karn
bouquets of white blossoms amidst figs
twined with perfumed smoke and spirit.
GAHHR GOOOOOHOOOOO SHROWNN NAH
AIEOOO THOOOOOR THE MATTER
of physique and blunted and sharpened grooon
of dishes and sticks blooohn esh ell thownie.
Everywhere oh my called on heart ! Everywhere !
Everywhere thou fried bindings.

YAHRHOOON NAHGROOOR OON MEEELT !
OOHN ESS TATH HAR FREEDOM.
GRAHHR ! GAHOOOOOOR GRAHH-GAHR !
The heavy curtains are raised
by roaring
upward flowing with implesharr grahh grace.
Blackness upon white and heavenly coloring
frahhn gahr groooh gahoor rahhr ! Grah !
Hrahhr thah noose eeelt em tell.
DROOOOOOOSHOOOON ! SHHROO-
OOOOO !
Fine green ferns amidst crevices
and wet trailing moss upon logs in streams !
Thah hoors ess freee.

I have called for thy roooring drohmeth nay blare
owth ooonshpraken. Oh pit of eye-tightening delight
above pink continents of darkness where island universes
float like sunsets o'er Los Angeles.
In the day now drooom nortath grahh harrrech.
EHH HOOOOOOH GRAHH ! GAHR !
GRAHGGR HRAHHR GAHHR AIEOOMETTER
TOOSH-GHRAA ! HRAHWW NARTROOOHM
RAHHR.
And I am still in awe
of the beast creatures
moving about me een el droooshoomahr
barr en lair tah droom — OH THOU !

OH CHILD, I LOVE THEE, THOU ART
TO ME AS SOME PARADISE
I WOULD HAVE FORGOTTEN.
Ten trillion animal ancestor angels sing of thy lost tooth
and the flashing light of thy cheeks and eyes.
OH ! OH ! OH ! TAHGROON STRANGENESS
heaping the mounts of thy being about thee
with cub brilliance, noog grahn toor
nah ess foorgoon thah tohr-troop naie-aieooo.
OOOH NAH-GREEEE OBLESH FINDING
what matters in the seedy vales.
And growing, sleeping, dancing.
OH, THY FACE & MOTIONS, OH !

DRAHN REEZER GRANN-LEEEP MOWR

stooon grahh drahhr toomowr thown yeee
bleesh nathoor coop stile peehn blash n'rooor
gahhr grahh gahoooor roooh grahhr
the brown silver grass-leaves in trillions — rustle
and move as fur of a vast breerth.
— The green spruce are hugging
ascending to a laughing leap.
Time & space whistle together where we
are non-mammalian
and our gahroon molecular voices yearn.
Brah theee ah hoool y'rahh thahrr ! *Thoo* !

Bleeezsh thahrr mah drooon ! Bleezsh marrr !
Oooh thowrr growrt-thanny. Again I have the thread
to thy breasts & head thou'st looorm deahrr.
OOHH MOWWRR THAHST DROOM !
I BLEASH MAHR NAHRGAHROOOOO
eem el esh tah-tooor norrog !
Many ! Many ! Oooh nah ay-ooh shmeeelt
toohr mool-tipals. Thah esh doohme-blythe
musk of thy drime thah varm sweeze musk
amongst all the barren & bright veils —
AH NOH OOOH YAH !
Roorahling pour thy thah thou sweeem bresh !
AHHR YAHHHHR !

Grahnthoooor the streaked dust upon glass !
Gharrgrooor the marks of the blurred rain !
Gahooool locorhahr the vast dead daily artifacts
and tracks reminiscent of thee !
GROWWHARR-BLEEESH THE SUNFLASH !
GLOOOOWL THE SPECKPASSAGE
AHH AHGG ! NAYAOH RAYIEE NROOOR-OHH.
Yeor naptorr droomsh thy reeng-toor.
Wahr ahn tell esh meetohr tah droohmm.
YAIEEE HEEEEAORRR !
YAAIIIEEEEE HEAYEEAOOORRR ! STOWH !
GROOOOOHM !

MOOOOOOOHR ROHRDRESH THOWTOOOR
GRAHM
MOOOOOHOOOL ENDRESH TAH !
GLOWL OOOH AHTEEEER MANGST
thah teeeen heeeereem eeorr mangst
ooohr lyings pon ooooh oooh oooohhdreshk.
Grhahh. Grahh-grahh grahgooooor aeeyor raharr.
Ah aieee thou oceanic thy heeer hooooom gahhr rooh
drooohmeeorshnathaktaye pooom-ohr
thy
bones and bosom
and mothered flesh
and all things becoming pixied life in this our continent
nahg cloohz.
RRROH !

In the molecular consciousness I reeeahah reeahoored
frah meee foornooze thah seeg wahbeeeng.
OH THOOOH ! AH ! OOOH !
AHND HEERT TOOTHOU EESARR.
Eeese ahl frooseen feeahr meh ? Nah, meer eekohrt
YAHH HAIEOW YAHHR HOOEESE!
Amidst the tall cool redwoods, icy the tall slim
heart threads thah manger ahn graharrr
eeem theorezeeling. Ooohn heer thah nooer . . .
OH ! NAY-OHHH ! EN MEEZ PREED !
— I breathing midst the honeysuckle locks
of thy hair like the hummingbird.

NOH RAYOR DOH RAHTREESH. I drew thee up
— cleaning the nerve tube — I practised
imaging for an instant that I controlled the Power
and felt movement from the 4th
to the 6th flower. I felt thee in full greyness
and saw the flutterings of figures & color.
The earth beneath was a monument
on which I sprawled in monumentality.
All was a vast lucidity of rarhrhooleeer
DRAHHSH KRAYRARR
NROOOZSH-THREEORT KRAHRR GAHR
GRAHH GAHARR N'ROHH HROHHR GRAHHR
AND ALL NOTES OF THE TOYFUL ABSOLUTE.

Sept. 19
In deep labor
thou memorensorium !
Each return a joyful surprise
without fail !

The hardest to see is that which lies beneath the eyes.
AHHG FOOOORNOOOOZE!
The hardest to hear is thy mohrest voice.
HRAHHG FOOOORNOOOOOOOOOZE !
AH THOW OHSHESHTY DRAHRRM NOOBREEETH
in the blue and pink glimmerrohrahrr meests.
Dayohh ! Howhrr ! Aye ! Aye thow aye !
In the blessing sunwarmth — *aye!* Where the robbers pass
beneath the visages of titans,
and the real sensualities melt before the higher
Aye ! *DROWWWW !* Aye !
AHHOHH DOW MOOOOSHTOREEEEEEN-
OWWRRR . . .

The beauteous face is blond rising from black velvet
out of gray
too thah drooohoooomorth dayah tah groww gahrr
ooooh neshk oooobreeorth sharamak
to the signed hands of love, where day is the pure horn
and blowing grash-morr kamarash
toooooo thoww nyorr ayorr blymeth reeeall aye yee ez
dromort grooometh nowwr-remetter ahh n'yohh
AND THE EAGLE PERCHED UPON THE NOSE
RAISES AND DIVES
into thah neeoreshity, blahsmah
woohmann — ayeeeohhr nakeahh ! THOWW !
YAH ! AYE ! MREEE-ESHTORR !

RAYGRAHAOHRR GRAHH THEESSH NEEORR
OH THOU OH MY OHBLEMISH
NAGRAHNTORR EKKGEOSH SWEETNESS
IM BLEEEMTHEORRT NAK THOWNY
bliss bleese gahrten shayohmok thahntoor
ogreosh-tarr grayhaorr kapituleem noherhorrtosh
gahrr grahh eem shayoreth drooogen thow
thy holy eternal nectar honey crystallized and congealed
in touch-scent o'er rolling roohrr nak grahh
rahhr graghrrr drayneeowtheen graghoooor
RAHHR GRAHHHHHHHR BLEEEELZE.
ROH !
Thy everest peeping — ahhh sweeeeze !

HRAHH ROWSH OHTREOBLAYMOTHE
thy deeern bayvow en ess ell taytorr my oh thy reeert
nohtrow groandorr toosheorr trayomayoth
grayowhrr grahooor-mek gahhr tamahhr thahroon
een thah kal wassoor oohnesh thyreen me-ohtrah.
Loh reesh thou droog fahss ooh myor dethty
shoon gahhhhr-grah gahr grah thee-owsh.
RAHRREEOHMAG-BLAYSHTOR NARR
SOOOOTHUMM
GAHHRGAHHHR GAHROOOOO HRAHHR
AH EEEEOHRRT HOWW NOOOOR GAHHR
and thy aye thy owthou brows and eyes
vast in air.

HROWSH NOWRRRRR THRAGEEEEE YAH
EFF LEW-VIOWSH TROWM NYARR THYEE.
In the emptiness thy face appearest upon the hills.
Ryesowtheeah nowrr bluegreen and touched
garrnoww. Oh thou noor thou deeven. Ghrahh !
Mirror of my absolute pale harmony made real
upon my knee droost toorm thah noh aye !
OHSH ! BLOWMM TARRR-THAHNTOH
oooobreosh tanthor in the multiple morns
nahg rooh bereengs from my own more than mehr.
SHOOOWEREEE RAHGRAYAYOAR !
RAHGRAYAYAY-HAYOARR ! NROH !
SHOOOOOOOOOOHN !

GRAHH GHARRR GAHROOOH GARR NOOOOO
GAHARRR GRAH GARRRRR NOOOOO SOOOOOM
GAHHR HRAH GRAYGHARR-GREEEE GARR
HRAHHRR GREEEHARRR NARGARROOOOO
GRRHH

thowert narr gahrooooh reeeheeer-grh gahrrr reeeheeerg
grahh garhoorm gah-gragahhr hrahhhrr tharr noon-grah ! !
Nye theeooort greee yah harhh grah hrah hroggrrh ! Raharrr !
Reeezooorn thowtow; grahh gahhrtheeort gahhr tathoorn
n'yeeer gahr grahaayoor gah hagrooor raharr grahh !
NYORT-GRAYHAOW ! GAH RAHARR
I RENOUNCE THEE THOWW LOVINGLY SWEEZE
MEER !

OH THEE THOOOO THOW NYARR GRAHAHH !
SWEEEREEZE MYTOOOR-DROWM GAHARRRR !
HAH-OOOH YAH FEERZE THAHNDING,
YAYOHH GAHRR GRAYRRR GAHRRR
GHRAHOOOOR
GAHAHHHR HRAGRAHARR GRAH GAHR.
OH I FEAR THE ENDING OF THY MY EYES
GRAHRR GAHHRHOOOOREENG
oohn bleesh thahn koortoon oohbleoayormesh.
THAH DROOON !
AND KNOWINGLY AWAIT IN TRIUMPH
thah doozsh eeeteorr thah hoolshwayze
oooohgahr thy clefts.

(in fear and trembling)

GRAHH HARR GAHHR HRAHH GOOOOOORHH!
GARHH GAHHHRRRR! GAHROOOOH, AYE!
GAHHR GAHRHOOO-RHEER GRAHAHH! OH
thah neert gahhr grahgmn grhh drt gahr grayhayoar
nyarr grooh hrahh grahrgmn grooor HAHHR!
GRAHIEE THOW VAROOM SENTIENT GAHRGRR
JOINER OF TIME, SPACE & GAHREEEOH
GAHHR-HOOOM NEORR GAHRRGRAGM HRAHRR.
AY HI MEOH GARGM GRAHHRR GAHOOOOO
THEEER GRAHDOON HROHH NYORR!
Gahr ghrmayorhrrr. Grayhoww no ooobleosh.
GAHHHHHR!
SEEEZMEOH-SHORNETT
GROOOOOOOOOOOOOOOOH! GAHRRR!

IN TRANQUILITY THY GRAHRR AYOHH
ROOHOOERING
GRAHAYAOR GAHARRR GRAHHR GAHHR
THEOWSH NARR GAHROOOOOOOOH GAHRR
GRAH GAHRRR ! GRAYHEEOARR GRAHRGM
THAHRR NEEOWSH DYE YEOR GAHRR
grah grooom gahhr nowrt thowtooom obleeomosh.
AHH THEEAHH ! GAHR GRAH NAYEEROOOO
GAHROOOOOM GRHH GARAHHRR OH THY
NOOOSHEORRTOMESH GREEEEGRAHARRR
OH THOU HERE, HERE, HERE IN MY FLESH
RAISING THE CURTAIN
HAIEAYORR-REEEEHORRRR
in tranquility.

LOVE
thy
! oh my oohblesh !

At the age of twenty-two Michael McClure gave his first poetry reading at the legendary Six Gallery event in San Francico where Allen Ginsberg first read *Howl*. He is the author of twenty-five books of poetry, most recently *Of Indigo and Saffron*, two novels, books of essays, and journalism in the *Rolling Stone* and *Vanity Fair*. He has received numerous honors including a Guggenheim fellowship and the Alfred Jarry Award. He created two TV documentaries. In the late Sixties his play *The Beard* instigated a successful censorship battle after the police arrested the actors of the Los Angeles production fourteen nights in a row. The play went on to receive two Obie awards and is performed across the U.S. and Europe. McClure's songwriting includes "Mercedes Benz" with Janis Joplin. With his friend Ray Manzarek, keyboardist of The Doors, McClure performed poetry and music on stages around the world.

Besides poetry and art, his deep interests are the biological environment and biology.

McClure describes himself as a mammal patriot and believes, in the words of Diane di Prima that, "the only war that matters is the war against the imagination."